'Unclassifiable. Classify under poetry, the

– Carolyn Lloyd Davies, Artistic Director

'The poems shake Shakespearean fragm

Lines separated from the hum of dialogue are revitalised in shimmering assemblages.'

– Emma Smith, Professor of Shakespeare Studies at Hertford College, Oxford.

'I love the idea of all the contradictions held in trying to begin something. And the idea of picking up a mangled matter and making a dream. In these pieces, the feeling of someone trying to express themselves from a position that feels impossible came across to me very powerfully.'

– Jane Fallowfield, Literary Manager, Royal Court Theatre, London.

'Superb! The line "I will play. I will say nothing. I will see what I can do" in *I Will Begin* really jumped out at me for the modulation of phrases and the juxtaposition of heightened and everyday language – it's a mesmerising effect used so well in these poems.'

– Luke Kennard, Poet, Professor of Creative Writing, Birmingham.

'Surprising and haunting.'

– Stephen Greenblatt, John Cogan Professor of the Humanities, Harvard.

Shakespeare Okuni

A Twist *of* Rotten Silk

or Words to That Effect

First published 2026
by Rowanvale Books Ltd
The Gate
Keppoch Street
Roath
Cardiff
CF24 3JW
www.rowanvalebooks.com

A CIP catalogue record for this book is available from the British Library.
Paperback ISBN: 978-1-83584-130-3
eBook ISBN: 978-1-83584-131-0

Printed and bound in Great Britain by Bell and Bain Ltd, Glasgow

A Twist *of* Rotten Silk

A Twist of Rotten Silk

Is it not a language I speak? I speak I know not what.
Dreaming of another world, and a better.
And what broken piece of matter.
Where am I? What world is this?
I know not where I am nor what I do.
Are these things spoken? Or do I dream? Or have I dreamed till now?
Is this a vision? Is this a dream? Do I sleep?
I do not sleep. I see, I hear, I speak.
I remember a mass of things, but nothing distinctly.
The dream's here still. Even when I wake it is.
Without me as within me. I see it feelingly –
A twist of rotten silk. A twist of rotten silk.

Beware My Follower

Beware my follower. All's cheerless, dark, and deadly.
Are you there with me? This feather stirs. I have a tree.
Stones have been known to move, and trees to speak.
O. Croak not, black angel, I have no food.
He that keeps nor crust nor crumb shall want some.
Here, father, take the shadow of this tree.
You are a spirit, I know. When did you die? Fa, sol, la, mi.
I had a wound here that was like a V.
But now 'tis made a double V. Another shape shall make me.
There's a thing within tells me. An O without a figure.
Crowned with rank fumiter and furrow-weeds –
Let's step into the shadows of these trees.

Brutish

Bastards and syllables. What I think I utter.
Bagot, Bushy, Green. Brown paper and old ginger.
Assist. A thing most brutish. I am not bookish.
Up with my tent. Up with the tent. Bring me the crown.
Give me my robes. Give me my robe. Bring me my crown.
Ha? A little bastard child? A little changeling?
Yes. Stand as if a person were author of herself.
Set the crown on the head of this forgetful person.
Then shall the realm of Albion come to great confusion.
All is uneven and left at six and at seven.
Bastards and syllables. Bagot and Bushy and Green.

Carcanet

A creature comes to me. The things it speaks it speaks to me.
What is my name? Am I that name? What name?
Carcanet. Call me Carcanet. Call me. And I will answer.
Can you remember? Do you remember? Will you remember?
Remember where you are? Remember who you are?
Remember your part? Remember when comes your cue?
Remember what I have said. Remember what I told you.
Remember me. Remember this. Remember. Yes.
Call me. And I will answer. Call me by my name.
Carcanet. Call me Carcanet. And I will come again –
A creature comes to me. The things it speaks it speaks to me.

Darkling

My stars shine darkly over me. My face I'll grime with filth.
Will you darkling leave me? O do not so. Oes and eyes of light.
I talk of dreams. I can hear my face. I think you can.
It is not night when I do see your face.
Therefore I think I am not in the night.
So. Quick bright things come to confusion.
Take my coloured hat and cloak. Oes and eyes of light.
This is the night. This thing of darkness. This, this.
Sons of utter darkness. Put out the light. And were left darkling.
So quick. Bright things come to confusion.
From the seedness to the teeming foison –
So quick bright things come to confusion.

Dear Creature I Have

Dear creature. I have a thing for you.
Dear creature. I can tell you one thing.
Dear creature. I can speak against.
Dear creature. The thing I say.
Dear creature. I cannot think.
Dear creature. I cannot sing.
Dear creature. I cannot say the words.
Dear creature. These are the words.
Dear creature. These are the words I think.
Dear creature. These are the words.
Dear creature. I will say for you.

Dear Creature You Are

Dear creature. You are the singer.
Dear creature. We will say our song.
Dear creature. These are the words.
Dear creature. These are the words I think.
Dear creature. Wild and whirling words.
Dear creature. I will say for you.
Dear creature. The thing I say.
Dear creature. I will say for you.
Dear creature. These are the words.
Dear creature. You are the singer.
Dear creature. We will say our song.

Here Is My Space

Here is my space. All things are in readiness.
Why do you make such faces?
I never saw you in my life till now.
What's the matter? Who am I? Ha?
What am I? Speak if you can.
What are you? Are you a comedian?
Ha. The citizens say not a word.
Beholders of this frantic play.
All things are in readiness.
Here could I breathe my soul into the air.
We must all part into this sea of air.

How Like a Dream

How like a dream is this I see and hear.
I am amazed and know not what to say.
Like a dull actor now I have forgot my part.
It is a part that I shall blush in acting.
Is this a prologue, or an epilogue?
Will you think of rotten kings or blubbered queens?
Simply the thing I am shall make me live.
I'll play the orator. La. My language.
Following darkness like a dream. Follow my voice.
I will not keep this form upon my head.
I will encounter darkness as a bride.

I Am a Feather

I am a feather. I am a fool. I am alone.
I am a magician. I am a messenger.
I am a soldier. I am a stranger here.
I am bound to speak. I am coming on.
I am directed by you. I am done. I am drawn in.
I am fire and air. I am for all waters.
I am for the air. I am found by you. I am full of lead.
I am giddy. I am glad. I am glad of it.
I am glad to see you. I am glad to see you mad.
I am glad to see you well. I am going. I am gone.
I am he. I am here. I am here to speak.

I Am Hers I Am His

I am hers. I am his. I am hurt. I am I.
I am in this. I am in this earthly world.
I am in this forest. I am in tune. I am left out.
I am light and heavy. I am like you they say. I am lost.
I am mad. I am meek and gentle. I am merry.
I am myself. I am myself alone. I am native here.
I am no such thing. I am not as I have been.
I am not here. I am nothing. I am not I.
I am not in the mind. I am not in the night.
I am not mad. I am not merry.
I am not of many words. I am not old. I am not sick.

I Am Not What I Am

I am not sorry. I am not very sick. I am not well.
I am not what I am. I am old. I am old and foolish.
I am one. I am one now. I am one of those.
I am on fire. I am out. I am out of service.
I am prepared. I am put to sea. I am quit.
I am ready. I am ready now. I am reckless.
I am resolved. I am rough. I am rough and lecherous.
I am sent on. I am sent to speak. I am she.
I am sick. I am sick and sullen. I am skilless.
I am so. I am sorry. I am so sorry.
I am sotted. I am sound. I am standing water.

I Am the Shadow

I am stiff and weary. I am strong and lusty.
I am stung. I am subdued. I am supposed dead. I am tame.
I am that flower. I am the dog. I am the sea.
I am the shadow. I am the thing I was.
I am too blunt and saucy. I am too childish-foolish.
I am too old. I am too young. I am undone.
I am very glad. I am very glad of it.
I am very sick. I am very sorry.
I am very well. I am well. I am wild. I am with child.
I am with you. I am young. I am yours.
I am yours for the walk. I am your shadow.

I Will Begin

I will begin. I will be gone. I will be silent.
I will do anything. I will do it. I will do nothing.
I will do such things. I will do this. I will do what I can.
I will keep my word. I will not keep my word. I will not sing.
I will not speak. I will not speak a word. I will perform it.
I will play. I will say nothing. I will see what I can do.
I will sing. I will sing it. I will tell it softly.
I will tell you. I will tell you a thing.
I will tell you the beginning. I will unclasp.
I will undo. I will undo myself. I will unmask.
I will use your skill. I will whisper. I will, I will, I will.

Kerelybonto

Throca movousus, cargo, cargo, cargo.
Cargo, cargo, cargo, villianda par corbo, cargo.
Boskos thromuldo boskos.
Boskos vauvado.
Kerelybonto.
Manka revania dulche?
Oscorbidulchos volivorco.
Acordo linta.
Porto tartarossa.
Bosko chimurcho.
Boblibindo chicurmurco.

Kickshaws

Kickshaws. Kickshawses.
In my cloak-bag is.
A box. A green box.
Feathers and papers.
Stones, touchstones, vials.
Kickshaws. Kickshawses.
A bundle of cloth.
A mantle. A cloak.
Gloves, scarves, and veils.
In my cloak-bag is.
Kickshaws. Kickshawses.

King and Queen

The king of Albion? A king of patches and shreds.
The queen of Albion? A queen of tatters and rags.
Are you a man? Are you a woman?
A queasy question. A queasy question.
This is the man. This is the woman.
I have seen him in England. I have seen him in France.
I have seen her in England. I have seen her in France.
Will the king and queen hear this piece of work?
You have broke it, cousin, and you will make it whole again.
Yes. You will piece it out with a piece of your performance.
Albion's king. Albion's queen. I will be king and queen.

My Crown

Where is my crown? Who took it from the cushion?
I'll have this crown of mine. I'll give away my crown.
The crown. I have the placing of the English crown.
Soldieress. I love your majesty. My crown. Put on my crown.
Stamp, rave, and fret, that I may sing and dance.
Will the king and queen hear this piece of work?
You will piece it out with a piece of your performance.
Where is the crown? Who took it from my cushion?
This herbwoman made you serve her both in person and in purse.
There, take the crown, and with the crown my curse.
I will proclaim myself what I am. And this cushion my crown.

Nettles and Strawberries

We cannot live on grass.
We will go walk a little in the orchard.
I saw some nettles in your garden.
I saw some strawberries in your garden.
I have sent for some of them.
For some of these. Nettles and strawberries.
We call a nettle a nettle, and a strawberry a strawberry.
Underneath the nettle grows the strawberry.
We will go walk a little in the orchard.
Omit nothing may give us aid.
Nettles and strawberries.

Play

Is there no play? A play there is.
What do I call the play?
A Forest of Feathers –
An old infant play a long time out of play.
I play the touch with a peacock's feather.
Can you play a forest of feathers?
Come, you'll play with me.
Prepare to play. I must have you play.
This play is the image of a forest of feathers.
Play something like a forest of feathers.
Play. I play. This play is playing.

Proclamation

A proclamation. Go, call the people. A crowd of people.
The proclamation. Go bring the rabble here to this place.
Youths that thunder at a playhouse and fight for bitten apples.
Rascal people. Slippery people. Mutinous people.
I shall do well. The people love me, and I love the people.
The qualities of people. And quietness of the people.
Hear me, people. Hear what I say. It is to you that I speak.
All the realm shall be in common. All things shall be in common.
There shall be no money. I thank you, people. It shall be so.
There's no more to be said. In the people's name it shall be so.
Proclamation. In the name of the people. It shall be so.

Recreation

Here I am. Here we are. There is a play.
It is a thing I made. It is a kind of history.
Admit me chorus to this history.
And then imagine me taking your part.
Admit me chorus to this history.
And all things change them to the contrary.
I am weak with toil, fabulous and false.
Sick in the world's regard, wretched and low.
A poor unminded outlaw sneaking home.
And where I did begin there shall I end.
And tears shed here shall be my recreation.

Snip

A thing of nothing. Note this before my notes.
There's not a note of mine that's worth the noting.
Here's snip, and nip, and cut, and slish and slash.
Like to a scissor in a barber's shop.
What reply, ha? To this tune, matter, and method?
Is the world as it was? Which is the way?
Is it sad and few words? Or how? The trick of it?
I had a thing to say, but will fit it with some better tune?
I had a thing to say, but let it go. Go, you thing, go.
I understand how all things go. You're like something that –
I know not what. 'Tis trash. Note notes, and nothing.

Spices, Ink, and Paper

Chaos is come again. Shall I have audience?
Take up this mangled matter at the best.
Dreaming of another world, and a better.
And what broken piece of matter.
Bring me spices, ink, and paper.
Dreams are toys. Even so. My tale is told.
I have performed my task. Go your ways and play. Go.
Your actions are my dreams. I have lost myself. My name is lost.
How far is it now to the end of the world?
Dreaming of another world and a better –
We shall know nothing here but one another.

Storical Pastoral

I'll tell you my dream. I remember the story.
The story of my life. The story of your life.
Industrious scenes of pribbles and prabbles.
Comedy, history, tragedy, pastoral. Pastoral.
Tragical pastoral. Pastoral.
Historical tragical pastoral. Pastoral.
Comical 'storical tragical pastoral. Pastoral.
Bitter, black, and comical. Pastoral.
Bitter, black, and tragical. Pastoral. Bitter and sweet.
Pastoral. New matter still. Pastoral. Rubbish and dust.
Pastoral. La, la, la, la. Pastoral – / Prepost'rous –

Sun Wheel Flower

And but for one thing I care for nothing –
And here I'll be and there I'll be –
And here again and there again –
And nothing brings me all things –
And nothing is impossible –
And that's nothing but it shall be –
And the sun has seen my folly –
And the wheel is come full circle –
And this I shall never do again –
And this only and no more –
And what sun wheel flower is this

Swerve

I swerve. I smirch my face with umber.
I have drunk and seen the spider.
I have forgiven and forgotten all.
I will do what I can for you all.
I clap my wings upon the table.
I play in one person many people.
In the field. In the town. In the temple.
I am a child. I am a spirit. I am invisible.
Herbwoman. Linguist. Soldieress.
I swerve. I smirch my face with umber –
It is not madness that I utter.

Teach Me

Teach me, dear creature, how to think and speak.
And here become as new into the world.
You look as you had something more to say.
Give me your hand. Have you no more to say?
Say. What is your will? What will this come to?
What will become of this? What will this do?
Let's see, let's see. Would you create me new?
Transform me, dear creature. Create me new.
Teach me, dear creature, how to think and speak.
These words, these looks, infuse new life in me.
Use me as you will. Utter more to me.

These Words

These words, these looks, infuse new life in me.
Teach me, dear creature, how to think and speak.
Give me your hand. Have you no more to say?
You look as you had something more to say.
Say. What is your will? What will this come to?
What will become of this? What will this do?
Let's see, let's see. Would you create me new?
Transform me, dear creature. Create me new.
Teach me, dear creature, how to think and speak.
And here become as new into the world.
For I am almost ready to dissolve.

This Abruption

Where am I? Where have I been? What country, friends, is this?
Am I in France? Are all the people mad? What is this?
Who is it that can tell me who I am? What am I?
What is the matter? What is here? What is he? What is she?
What's he? What's she? What's here? What's the matter? What's the matter here?
What stuff's here? What are you there? Your names? What are you? Your name?
Where do you live? Who are you? Who is here? Who's here? Who's there?
Who comes here? Who have we here? What shall I do?
What should I do I do not? What will you do? What would you do?
What would you have me do? What would you have me do? What's that?
What's the news? What's the news? What's the news with you?

This Is and Is Not

This is and is not cressid.
I eat root. I love Aliena.
In Lipsbury. In the ventricle of memory.
I have told you what I have seen and heard.
The things that I have seen and heard.
Obscured in the circle of this forest.
Obscured in the circle of this island.
It's past the size of dreaming.
This is and is not cressid.
This is the silliest stuff that ever I heard.
In Lipsbury. I the matter will reword.

Undone

Are we undone, cast off, nothing remaining?
All broken implements of a ruined house?
We are undone. We are all undone.
Are you a man? Are you a woman?
You must forget to be a man.
You must forget to be a woman.
We know each other well. We know nothing.
We are undone, cast off, nothing remaining.
We must disguise ourselves. We must do something.
We will do it. We will mutiny. We will play our part –
Be quiet, people. Be quiet and depart.

Velcome

Fa, sol, la, mi. Fa, sol, la, mi.
Velcome, Marcadé. Plant a pyramid.
Vat is you sing? I do not like dese toys.
Go and vetch me a box, a green-a box.
Do intend vat I speak? A green-a box.
Fa, sol, la, mi. Fa, sol, la, mi.
I must be ripped. To pieces with me.
I heard a humming which did awake me.
Welcome, Marcadé. What is it you seek?
My ancient incantations are too weak.
Wheak, wheak, wheak, wheak, wheak.

A Twist of Rotten Silk

Is it not a language I speak? I speak I know not what.
Dreaming of another world, and a better.
And what broken piece of matter.
Where am I? What world is this?
I know not where I am nor what I do.
Are these things spoken? Or do I dream? Or have I dreamed till now?
Is this a vision? Is this a dream? Do I sleep?
I do not sleep. I see, I hear, I speak.
I remember a mass of things, but nothing distinctly.
The dream's here still. Even when I wake it is.
Without me as within me. I see it feelingly –
A twist of rotten silk. A twist of rotten silk.

فتلة حريرٍ عفنة

أليست هذه لغة أحكيها ؟ أحكي ولا أدري ما أحكي .
أحلم بعالم آخر ، وأفضل .
ويا لها من مادة ممرقة هشة .
أين أنا وأي عالم هذا ؟
لا أعلم أنا أين ولا ماذا أفعل .
أليس هذا كلام يحكى ؟ أم أني أحلم ؟ أم أني كنت أحلم حتى الآن ؟
أهذه رؤيا ؟ أهذا حلم ؟ هل أني نائم ؟
اني لا أنام . أرى ، أسمع ، أحكي .
أتذكر الكثير من الأشياء، ولكن لا شيء تحديداً .
الحلم ما زال هنا . إن استيقظت فهو هنا .
من دوني وفي داخلي . أراه بكل حواسي .
فتلة حريرٍ عفنة . فتلة حريرٍ عفنة .

A Twist of Rotten Silk

Is it not a language I speak?
I speak I know not what.
Dreaming of another world, and a better.
And what broken piece of matter.
Where am I? What world is this?
I know not where I am nor what I do.
Are these things spoken? Or do I dream? Or have I dreamed till now?
Is this a vision? Is this a dream? Do I sleep?
I do not sleep. I see, I hear, I speak.
I remember a mass of things, but nothing distinctly.
The dream's here still. Even when I wake it is.
Without me as within me. I see it feelingly –
A twist of rotten silk. A twist of rotten silk.

腐りかかった絹の捻れた糸を

これはわたしが話せる言葉ではないのか?
何の話をしているのか、自分も知らない。
これと違う、これよりいい世界の夢を見ているよ。
壊れたものの破片。
ここはいったいどこだろう?どの世界?
どこにいるか、何をしているか、自分も知らない。
言葉から生じたのか?夢を見ているのか?今まで見ていたのか?
これはただの幻?ただの夢?今も寝ているのか?
いや、寝ていないだろう。目が見える、耳が聞こえる、声が話せる。
たくさんのことを思い出せるけど、どれも曖昧な記憶だけ。
夢はまだ消えていない。目覚めてもまだここにある、
わたしの中にも周りにも。切ない視線が触れている、
腐りかかった絹の捻れた糸を。腐りかかった絹の捻れた糸を。

Emma Smith
The Dialogue Continues

Enter Thersites with a letter for Achilles. Achilles doesn't name him but demeans him: 'Fragment!' The term and the tone are dismissive. The same slur recurs in *Troilus and Cressida*, when a spurned Troilus describes Cressida's love as 'the fragments, scraps, the bits and greasy relics' given to Diomedes, just as Antony insults Cleopatra by calling her 'a fragment / cold upon dead Caesar's trencher.' Fragments here are shop-soiled, fingered, bearing the marks of previous use. In the case of Cressida and Cleopatra, the notion is rendered abject in gendered terms, applied to women regarded as venal or even venereal rather than virginal. In the case of Thersites, the notion is rendered abject in social terms, applied to a man regarded as a subhuman parasite. When Coriolanus erupts against the populace at the beginning of his play, he bids them 'Go get you home, you fragments'.

But fragments, in Shakespeare Okuni's sense, are more generous and more generative. The poems here are less concerned with where these bits have been, or with sending them home. Instead, the fragment is like a welcome migrant, able to do something new in her new home.

Some of that novelty is linguistic. Cut out from larger structures of Shakespearean language, the phrases here have a strong aural quality. These are poems for the voice as much as for the page, for performance as much as for reading.

Okuni notices how words chime: 'Pastoral – / Prepost'rous', 'Bagot, Bushy, Green. Brown paper and old ginger'.

It's no surprise that some of these poems have been set to music: they are like variations that replay and reimagine themes, melodies, and voices. The poems shake Shakespearean fragments into shifting, prismatic patterns. Lines separated from the hum of dialogue are revitalised in shimmering new assemblages. Words that were familiar become unfamiliar through repetition: 'I am', 'Dear creature', 'La, la, la, la'. Words that were strange become stranger: 'Kickshaws. Kickshawses', 'pribbles and prabbles'. Rhetorical figures of repetition and variation choreograph the internal movement of meaning, as denotation and connotation shift with the metamorphic quality of a chromatic cadence.

Spun from materials drawn from all thirty-eight plays, the fabric of these poems is tightly woven. Fragments here are in no way ragged, accidental, or imperfect. Unlike the vision of shattered sculpture or of terracotta shards curated in European museums, other modes of creative reuse – like quilting or the Japanese art of kintsugi – are closer to the method and outcome here. The great work of being made and remade, released in different forms, able to circulate and cross-pollinate, continues in these pieces.

My training as an academic Shakespearean always prompts me to trace these repurposed phrases back to the plays they come from. Believe me, it is a very pleasurable thread to follow, finding lines that are typically overlooked alongside others that would pass unnoticed in most readings or performances, and hearing the plays recombine and recognise each other in new conversations.

Take the collection title, *A Twist of Rotten Silk*. As the rough martial agon of *Coriolanus* reaches its brutal climax, Aufidius, the rebel general, speaks scornfully to his old foe whose defection to their cause has worn thin. Under pressure from his wife and his mother, Coriolanus has agreed not to lead the army against the city of Rome. It is, as he knows, a fatal concession. He has, says Aufidius, broken 'his oath and resolution like / A twist of rotten silk' (5.6.113-

4). The soldiers turn on Coriolanus, and stab him. A terrible final stage direction in the 1623 Folio announces his fall, and a last ignominy. 'Aufidius stands on him'.

The image of the rotten twist of silk in its dramatic context is thus both exotic and debased, luxurious and broken. It is a model of tragedy in miniature, where something noble and of great value becomes corrupted beyond recovery. It stands for Coriolanus's curdled pride, the failing that fatally turns his homeland against him.

But it also opens this play – and the collection that reclaims and repurposes the phrase – out to a larger world. Just as Coriolanus leaves Rome for the coastal rebel stronghold Antium, so the play is on the move, turning its glance eastwards, to the routes by which silk and other luxury goods reached Shakespeare's London. After generations of discussions of Tudor England as, in Shakespeare's own words, 'this sceptered isle', today's scholarship is concerned with revealing Tudor England's deep connections with the wider world through trade, translation, and migration. Spices, ideas, and stories were all trafficked through the great port of London, where the theatre that nourished Shakespeare's imagination overlooked the tidal river Thames, staging real, exotic, and imaginary worlds under the evocative name of the Globe.

'What world is this?' asks Shakespeare Okuni in the opening poem that gives its title to the collection. 'A Twist of Rotten Silk' returns at the end, resolving and dissolving in Lebanese and Japanese translations. The concerns of Coriolanus around belonging, alienation and empire are shifted into a different key; we are now in the wandering world of Pericles, an exiled prince whose journeys around the Mediterranean attempt to find what has been lost and to heal what has been broken.

So, seen in this way, the fragment still has an indexical relationship to the whole from which it is extracted. It is defined, to some extent, by the larger corpus, and it can never float entirely free of its connotations within its own playtext, always in the wake of the larger work. Making these phrases resonate with their initial context as well as their new one is an act of reverberative amplification. Because the collection is not a dictionary of quotations, it also reimagines the significance of the whole in ways that have a long history.

Early readers of Shakespeare were not committed to the aesthetic unity and completion of the plays. Rather, as contemporary documents show, readers identified and repurposed lines and phrases that were meaningful to them and which, crucially, did not need the entire scaffolding of the dramatic context to be communicative. They focused in on elements of the play's language that were already quotable or transferable, or made them quotable and transferable through selection.

This highly valued humanist activity of reading and of carrying over the chosen elements into a notebook for future use in conversation, correspondence or other compositions was known as *common-placing*. Usually these common-placed snippets lost their specific markers of time or place. Proper names, or deictic markers like 'this' or 'here' were omitted to make them more portable across texts. In a few cases, the original author was credited with the transported text, sometimes in order to secure its value. But mostly the fragments were semi-autonomous, living new lives, rearranged into different textual structures, newly provisional and echoic.

Reading *A Twist of Rotten Silk* by tracing phrases back to their source is only one way of considering these capacious poems, and a potentially limiting and ahistorical one. These fragments do not look backward to the imaginary plenitude of their source, but forward to their freedom. After all, there are no footnotes or endnotes in these pages, no citations, no suggested further reading. This is not – happily in that respect – Eliot's 'The Waste Land'. William Shakespeare's name is not mentioned. We are not prompted to read these as a commentary on his plays, we do not need to be experts in quotation-spotting or to bring an encyclopaedic knowledge of Shakespeare's works to our reading. Our author is not showing off.

Instead, phrases jostle, sometimes half-remembered, sometimes unique, sometimes reframed through juxtaposition. 'I will encounter darkness as a bride', 'Who is it that can tell me who I am', 'And this cushion my crown'. Some of them carry a Shakespearean strangeness, others are strikingly everyday. Words and phrases cut loose from their original context have the anthropomorphic opportunity to take a new deep breath. They are reset and re-sent into the world, not ancient but recent. At times, the poems may appear obliquely recognisable in the form of their source: on the page, the repeated eleven-line stanzas resemble Shakespeare's sonnets – traditionally fourteen lines – but they are not. In this foreshortened form, they hold back on the impulse to completion. Okuni offers a textual kaleidoscope where mirrored and refracted symmetries create something both obliquely recognisable and giddily new.

Holding back on the impulse to completion is one of the great qualities of this work. Writing of the vogue for fragments in the Romantic period, when Keats published 'Hyperion, a Fragment', and picturesque ruins were on everyone's bucket list, the critic Anne Janowitz writes that 'the fragment form becomes the place where the theme of incompletion is enacted'.

That idea of incompletion can seem strangely at odds with the centuries of Shakespearean appreciation and adulation, much of which has combined to build Shakespeare's perfect completeness, in the many editions of his 'Complete Works'. The plenitude of Shakespeare's œuvre can seem overwhelming, impenetrable, unapproachable even. Performing the roles is, as one knight of the English theatre recently put it, like climbing Mount Everest. A fragmentary Shakespeare is much more available, much less off-putting than a statuary one. Replacing this literary monument with something more granular – sampling the whole via parts, and substituting parts for the whole – offers a generous space to think more about creativity as an endlessly renewing process. Not a canonic space but a synchrotronic space.

If Shakespeare is valuable in our global world, it must be in large part because of the ability of these four-hundred-year-old plays to catalyse new interpretations and new invention. We need to level the monumental mountain – educationally, socially, culturally, textually – and, as here, creatively.

The Elizabethans have shown us the way. The word *common-placing*, in this sense, suggests not something everyday or commonplace, but a resource placed in common, to be held in common. These poems are just such commonplaces. Shakespeare Okuni's poems democratise Shakespeare's plays by rendering them as an available vocabulary across time and space. Here, the fragment makes the theme of incompletion visible, and available. One Shakespeare meets, and reframes, another, across time and space. The dialogue continues.

Acknowledgements

'I Will Begin' and 'Spices, Ink, and Paper' first appeared in *Wasafiri: International Contemporary Writing Magazine, Issue 107: Crisis/Recovery,* Autumn 2021, under the editorship of Malachi McIntosh and with the assistance of Emily Mercer.

Shakespeare Okuni

Shakespeare Okuni practised with Footsbarn Travelling Theatre and the Werdyn Gypsy Horse Circus before running away from the circus to act out and direct in England, France, Ghana, and Lebanon. He is the author of *Black Box*, a play for the actors of the National Theatre of Ghana, and *Mabinogion*, a libretto for string quartet, flute, and storyteller. With *The Dreaming Chorus*, a series of devised theatre workshops, he is developing a new piece drawn from William Shakespeare's unsettled plays.

Contents

Publisher Information

Rowanvale Books provides publishing services to independent authors, writers and poets all over the globe. We deliver a personal, honest and efficient service that allows authors to see their work published, while remaining in control of the process and retaining their creativity. By making publishing services available to authors in a cost-effective and ethical way, we at Rowanvale Books hope to ensure that the local, national and international community benefits from a steady stream of good quality literature.

For more information about us, our authors or our publications, please get in touch.

www.rowanvalebooks.com
info@rowanvalebooks.com